Introduction to Zen

Living With Less

Enrique Fiesta

Mendon Cottage Books

JD-Biz Publishing

All Images Licensed by Fotolia and 123RF.

Our books are available at

1. Amazon.com

2. Barnes and Noble

3. Itunes

4. Kobo

5. Smashwords

6. Google Play Books

Table of Contents

Introduction

The contemporary man is often at unease. Despite the significant advances in technology, rises in material standards of living, and the license to do almost whatever one pleases he is never at peace with himself and his surroundings. He rarely has the time to pursue peace.

His schedule is hectic, he is constantly pestered by the demands of an incessant and all-enveloping communication network, and his work is rote and routine. His existence is functionary, tasteless, and uncreative.

If this reminiscent of your experience of life, you need not feel ashamed. It is the plague of the contemporary and secular world. Our ancestors, despite unimaginable hardships, lived in a world populated by gods, spirits, ritual, and poetry. Their often agricultural lives revolved around the seasons, their sailors looked to the stars for directions, and their holidays (holy-days etymologically) were days of worship and celebration of the mysteries and glory of life. Everything in their world was rife with ultimate and hierarchic significance-everyone from the peasant to the king knew their place in the world, their relation to their fellow man, and their duties to their gods or God (*anno domini*).

Unfortunately, the industrial and scientific revolutions have removed the superficial air of mystery that permeated nature and the core of experience. Capitalism's re-evaluation of values and objects according to their utility and quantifiability made things like comfort, entertainment, and usefulness more "valuable" than non-quantifiable values like beauty, courage, and valor. Our technology has estranged us from nature and our jobs lack the color and beauty of the ancient craftsmen and farmers. It seems as though we have become slaves to a technical bureaucratic system that should be serving us!

I have written this short text in the hope that it will bring peace, creativity, and serenity to your life. I do not expect that it will be the answer to all of your questions or problems in this life. I merely hope that it *lead you* to deepen your experience of reality, focus your attention, and cultivate your person. The pursuit of peace and serenity is one that, happily, is up to each of us individually to uncover through trial and error, or less painfully, through wisdom and insight. May you use this text to your advantage. *Deo gratias*.

History of Zen

Zen is considered to be an evolution of Buddhist practice. Zen acquired its own unique shape and distinctness from other developments of Buddhism because it was filtered through Chinese thought as it spread from India via the Silk Road into China. The school of thought which particularly influenced what would become Zen Buddhism was Taoism. Unlike Western systems of thought, whose contours were shaped by a rigorous dialectic, formal logic, intense categorization, and anthropomorphism; the Taoist perspective is defined, or rather rooted in impression and spontaneity. The Taoists believed that man's role in the universe was to experience "the Tao"- the ineffable and flowing source of all things that exist. One had to find one's balance in order to be at peace in the universe. One could not attain this balance through effort, thought, or action- rather it could only be achieved through "non-action."

Buddhist doctrines, such as attempting to discover one's inner nature and the elimination of desire in order to be at peace in the universe, synergized with the Chinese and Taoist perspectives. The synthesis of the two doctrines emerged as Chan- a distinct form of Chinese Buddhism. Chan travelled to Japan and became "Zen"- which is the Japanese pronunciation of the Chinese word "Chan."

Principally, Zen is distinct from other forms of Buddhism from other forms of Buddhism because of its focus on achieving its aims- namely meditation. The Zen Buddhists attempt to flow into the river of experience and gain direct-insight into the nature of reality (the "really real") through said meditation. Its principal practice is called "Zazen" which literally means "sitting." See next chapter.

Zen is a practice most Westerners and newcomers to Zen advocate as a way to "simplify" their life. It is more akin to a re-orientation of one's perspective than a simplification of a lifestyle, though perhaps the consequences flowing from the re-orientation of mind bear the resemblances of so-called simplifications- such as attentiveness to what matters, economy, creative endeavors, so called naturalness, peace of mind, etc- and for the taxed, over-communicative, and apathetic Westerner, all these things are refreshing reprieves from the drudgery of everyday living...

The change in perspective that generally accompanies Zen practice is derived from practice's emphasis on focus. The Zen practitioner's newfound focus, or attentiveness, becomes an impression on the character of that person. This means that the Zen practitioner's focus becomes something natural to him- that he does not have to exert effort to bring to the fore. The focus is non-rational and spontaneous. Though Zen defies any attempt at categorization, definition, or limitation I tend to think of Zen in this way: if we look at the birds, at trees, or even at rocks, we unvaryingly find that the birds, trees, and rocks are all able to be themselves without exertion, effort, or complaint. We, on the other hand, often find ourselves depressed, confused, and bored. The patterns in nature, on the other hand, never seem to be bored of being themselves. The birds sing the same songs, the trees grow and shed their leaves every season, and the stones seem perfectly content. They are constant. The goal of Zen is to make man like the varied and wonderful forms of nature- constant and content with being what he is.

Zazen

At the heart of Zen practice is a method of meditation called zazen. Zazen literally means "sitting meditation." It is really a simple meditation, but it can be challenging to perfect it. The Zen Buddhists have, over the course of hundreds of years, established certain ways of sitting as being optimal for Zen practice. The purpose of this meditation is to achieve direct insight into the nature of reality, normally by clearing the mind of images and thoughts so that one's attention is focused on the ever-present moment.

The first step, though, is to find a place to practice zazen. The area chosen should be quiet and peaceful. There are different schools of thought regarding which areas are preferable, whether it be inside or outside, confined or spacious, but for our purposes one should just find a quiet area where one can sit comfortably. One should not bring a phone or have the television on when one practices zazen, as this distracts from the meditation and returns one's attention to the objects which gave rise for the need of zazen in the first place.

Traditionally, the Buddhist monks would practice zazen in a meditation hall called a *zendo*. To make the experience more comfortable, the monks sat on a cushion called a *zafu*, which itself was placed upon a mat called a *zabuton*. It is recommended that you purchase these materials, or something similar, because long periods of sitting on the floor, especially if it is hard, can be uncomfortable and even painful. Loose, comfortable clothing should be worn during zazen. Constricting or otherwise uncomfortable clothing will only be distracting.

The next step is to learn how one should sit. Posture is very important in zazen practice. The posture of zazen is seated, with folded legs and hands, and an erect but settled spine. The hands are generally folded together into a simple *mudra* over the belly and rested upon one's feet or legs. See below a picture of the *mudra*.

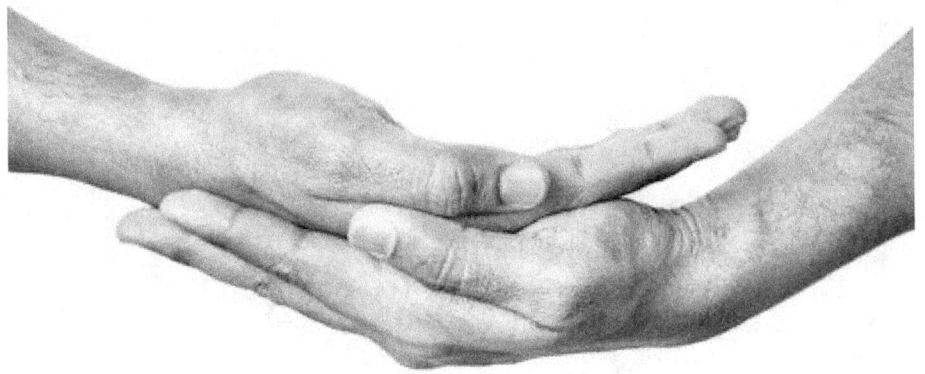

YOGA

Bhairav mudra

Gesture for meditation
and pranayama

The Zen typically practice zazen in one of several standard sitting styles. The first is the full-lotus position. This position is very difficult to attain without a great degree of flexibility. See below picture.

The half-lotus position is easier to attain, and is recommended if the full-lotus is impracticable. See below picture.

There is also the Burmese position. See below picture.

The last position is called the *seiza* position. This is a traditional Japanese sitting style. A pillow (*zafu*) is typically placed between the buttocks and feet to enhance comfort.

In addition, it is not uncommon for modern practitioners to practice zazen in a chair, often with a wedge or cushion on top of it so that one is sitting on an incline, or by placing a wedge behind the lower back to help maintain the natural curve of the spine.

Once an appropriate posture is achieved it is necessary to correct one's breathing. Breathing is an integral part of zazen. When you sit down into your chosen position, gently rock the body back and forth in decreasing arcs until your breath is settled in the *hara*, the body's center of gravity. It is located near the lower abdomen. One should have one's hands folded in the *mudra*, the mouth should be closed, and the tongue pressed onto the upper palate (the roof of your mouth). You should be breathing through your nose. Orient your attention toward your breath- attend to the breath- experience the breath.

仁者樂山

Due to our hectic, modern lifestyles achieving the perfect zazen state can be a challenge. Here is advice for how to attend to the breath and let go of distracting thoughts and images. Begin by counting every inhalation and exhalation as you breathe up to the number ten. Only count at the end of each inhalation and exhalation. Once you reach the number 10 repeat the process. If your mind begins to wander, become aware of it then attend to the counting and breathe again and begin your count at 1. As you practice, you will discover that you are able to count consistently to 10 without interruption. Once you believe you have achieved this level of proficiency, you should then cease to count only the exhalations.

The counting is a tool which allows you to discover when you have lost your attention to the breath. As you practice, you will develop a habit and the practice will become easier. With diligence, you will find that counting is no longer even necessary and that you can commence zazen at will.

As you abandon the breath, devote your being to the breath- in other words, *be* the breath. Breathe without effort, and effortlessly breathe. Do not rush the breath. Another variation of this practice is to repeat a *mantra*. This is sometimes equated to an Orthodox Christian practice called *hesychasm* wherein the practitioner, in order to avoid images and thoughts would repeat a single imageless word every time he noted his attention drifting. In either case, it is important to clear the mind and focus on your breathing.

Koans

Though zazen is the core of Zen practice, there is another method used by practitioners for achieving direct insight into the nature of reality- *Koan* reading. *Koan* is Japanese for "public case." It is analogous to a legal case presented in court. The origins of Koans are obscure, but it is likely they emerged from Chinese literary puzzles.

Part of the appeal of Zen practice to the Western imagination, is its seemingly mysterious nature. In an era where precision, exactness, and scientific certitude and skepticism dominates, the soul sometimes longs for simpler times and intuition. Koan practice is roughly an intuitive, non-discursive form of meditation or thinking (or non-thinking, since Zen meditation is adverse to images and linear thinking).

A Koan is a story, narrative, dialogue, or short saying that defies rational explanations. The purpose of the Koan is to force the Zen practitioner to engage in non-thinking, or to achieve direct insight into the nature of reality, rather than rely upon discursive and linear thinking. The most famous Koan to the West is, "What is the sound of one hand clapping?"

The Western misconception regarding the Koan is that it is a meaningless phrase or an unanswerable question. Though there is no correct or one answer, the purpose of Koan is clear- to break the Zen practitioner's reliance on fixed concepts, images, and assumptions about reality. It should also be noted that the Koan is not a riddle with a clever answer. Most of us are acquainted with the Sphinx's riddle, "what walks on all fours in the morning, two in the day, and three in the evening?" to the hero Oedipus. The riddle is distinct. The riddle requires one to *think* creatively- the koan demands no such thing. Zen is not creativity. As I mentioned before, Zen practice directs us to the path of being what we are- just like the birds, trees, and the stars.

Birds do not need to be creative to be birds, they need simply be. The koan leads the practitioner to simply be-ing in the present moment.

Although traditionally koan practice was conducted between an experienced Zen master and a student, in the West, where there is a shortage of Zen masters, the koan has become a predominately individual activity. It is likely a great advantage to receive feedback from a master regarding responses (or non-responses) to a koan, it may still be worthwhile to engage the koan individually. Do not try to invent a clever answer or attempt to be original- these are sure signs that one's ego is detracting from one's Zen practice. You are not the sum of reality. Let go of your ego, conceptions, and limitations and engage the koan with an earnest spirit.

Here are a few Koans with sample responses following. Try to discover a response yourself first before looking at the sample responses with explanations.

How do you make Mount Fuji take three steps?

How do you pick up a stone in a deep river without getting one's hands wet?

How do you hold a plough with empty hands?

Why is it not our tongue that we speak with?

Sample Responses:

Take three steps. Three steps are three steps no matter who takes them.

You reach in and pick up the stone. How else would you retrieve the stone?

Just pick up the plough. Do not bother about whether your hands are empty or not.

Say something. Just show that you are speaking.

If you do not like koan practice, do not bother with them. They are not essential to Zen practice. Just focus on zazen.

Zen Arts

From Zen practice emerged very distinct forms and methods of art, ritual, and ceremonies which have resonated with the Western mind ever since their discovery. There were incredibly talented Zen artists in Japan who practiced arts including poetry, origami, the tea ceremony, painting, calligraphy, music, and gardening. I will briefly discuss some of the arts appropriated by or used by the Zen artists.

First, it is helpful to distinguish the Zen aesthetic from the Western. The Westerner's approach to crafting beautiful objects, scenes, or spaces can be likened to an imposition. The Western mind encounters an object, lacking in beauty and grace, and he imposes form and order upon it in order to make it beautiful and attractive. The Zen mind seeks to impose nothing on objects or scenes… the Zen mind seeks to discover the essence or "thisness" of an object by cutting and clearing away what is not essential to the object. These two pictures show the distinction between a Western garden and an Eastern Zen garden- the former is Western, the latter Zen.

In the Western garden, forms have been imposed on the landscape. Sharp right angles divide the paths from the greens. Geometric forms of the same size and shape are cut into the greens. A pond has been artificially placed into the center of the garden. The beauty of the scene comes the creative balancing of pleasing shapes, orderly arrangement, and precision. The beauty of the scene comes less from the nature of the garden, than from the beauty of what the human mind can accomplish. The scene is precise, orderly, and mathematic.

The Eastern garden's beauty emerges from an entirely different source: the natural environment. We are not perceiving the beauty of geometry, mathematic precision, or order; rather, we are witnessing the serenity of the scene revealed through the process of elimination. No forms were imposed on the scene- the artists merely found a natural scene and trimmed away what was inessential. The trees are not uniform, the paths curve, and the plants are of a different species; none of these characteristics are present in the Western garden.

The Zen Buddhists applied this approach to all of their artistic endeavors. The pursuit of 'direct-insight' of the nature of reality and the elimination of fixed mental concepts and images can be felt from the simplicity and stillness of their arts.

The Haiku, for instance, allows only for a limited expression. Its limitations require the artist to express the bare essence of their object- as the lack of space does not allow a wealth of description. This can easily be contrasted with Western poetry. We derive our heritage from Homer, whose poetry was filled with enchanting descriptions of various scenes and objects. The Zen Buddhist, on the other hand, eliminates the details in order to arrive at the essence of the object.

Origami is another art Zen Buddhists typically practice and it is not surprising to see why. The practitioner begins with a square piece of paper and is permitted only to use that one, individual object to craft something beautiful. The beauty of the object is brought out of the paper, rather than it being imposed upon the paper. Anyone who has seen the grace of a paper crane has experienced the beauty of the Zen mind. I highly recommend origami to anyone wishing to practice an interesting craft which always results in a beautiful object.

The Japanese Zen rock garden is a "garden" composed of sand, rocks, moss, pruned trees and bushes to create a miniature landscape. The artist uses a rake to create "ripples" in the sand so as to give the sand the likeness of water. If you do not have the space, time, or energy to create a full-size Zen garden, one can fill a shoe-box lid with sand and craft a miniature rake out of tooth picks. You can find stones or any other object to decorate your mini Zen Garden and use the rake to make rivers, ponds, ripples, or whatever else you like. It can even become a part of your zazen practice if you decide to take breaks in between sessions. The raking can be quite relaxing and methodical.

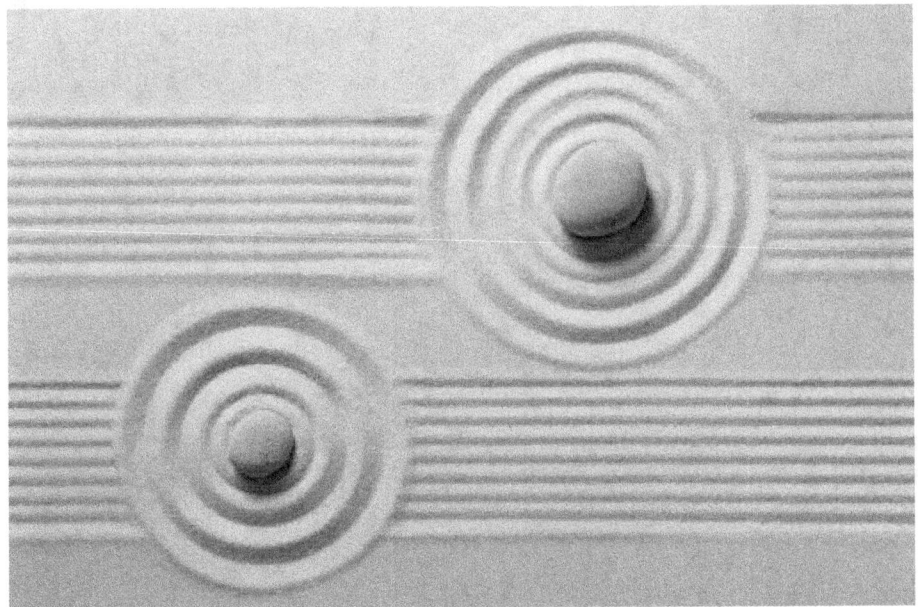

Conclusory Remarks

I hope you enjoyed this text and that you use it to your advantage. Zen practices can be quite relaxing and peaceful. Remember not to boast about being "into Zen" or to pretend to have attained spiritual heights due to your limited experience with Zen. The Zen practices, from zazen to the arts, are explored in this text only in a mode necessary to introduce Westerner's to practices which can help clear the mind, promote creativity, and help one step outside our often functionary existence. Please read more titles in the "Living with Less" series if you wish to learn about other approaches to economical and, hopefully, humane living.

Author Bio

Enrique Fiesta

I live in Southwest Florida and I enjoy studying the liberal arts, especially poetry and philosophy, attending Mass, and reading the classics. I studied Latin and Greek language and literature at university and I am currently pursuing a degree in law.

Our books are available at

1. Amazon.com
2. Barnes and Noble
3. Itunes
4. Kobo
5. Smashwords
6. Google Play Books

Check out some of the other JD-Biz Publishing books

Gardening Series on Amazon

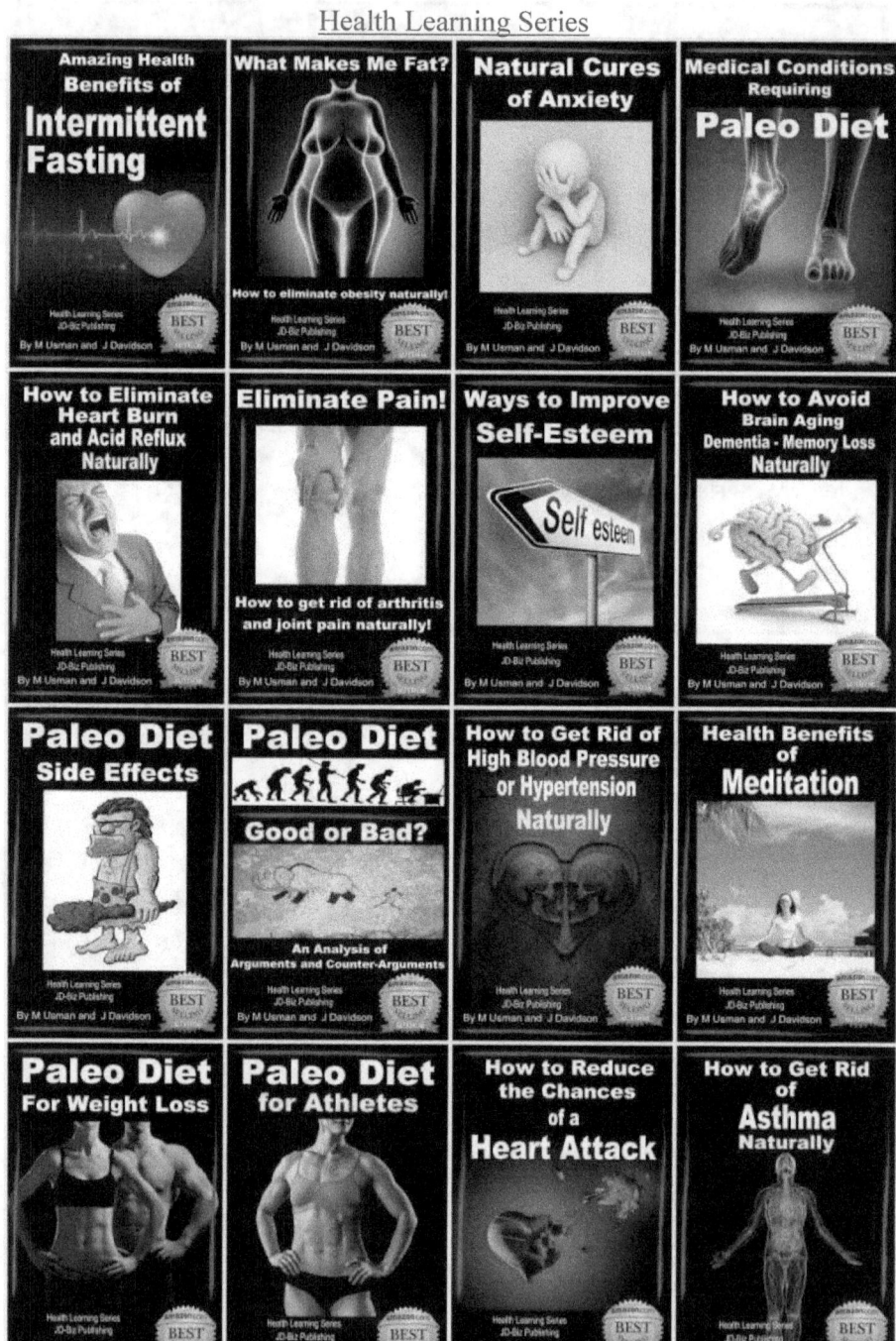

Learn To Draw Series

How to Build and Plan Books

Entrepreneur Book Series

Publisher

JD-Biz Corp

P O Box 374

Mendon, Utah 84325

http://www.jd-biz.com/

Mendon Cottage Books

P O Box 374, Mendon Utah 84325

www.ingramcontent.com/pod-product-compliance
Lightning Source LLC
Chambersburg PA
CBHW061931280526
45787CB00004B/1564